Time to Estimate

By Betsy Franco

Consulting Editor: Gail Saunders-Smith, Ph.D.
Consultants: Claudine Jellison and Patricia Williams,
Reading Recovery Teachers
Content Consultant: Johanna Kaufman,
Math Learning/Resource Coordinator of the Dalton School

Yellow Umbrella Books

an imprint of Capstone Press
Mankato, Minnesota

Yellow Umbrella Books are published by Capstone Press
151 Good Counsel Drive, P.O. Box 669, Mankato, Minnesota 56002
www.capstonepress.com

2 3 4 5 6 7 08 07 06 05 04 03

Library of Congress Cataloging-in-Publication Data
Franco, Betsy.
    Time to estimate/by Betsy Franco.
    p. cm.—(Math)
    Includes index.
    Summary: Text and photographs introduce everyday uses for estimation.
    ISBN 0-7368-1288-1
    1. Estimation theory—Juvenile literature. [1. Estimation theory.] I. Title. II. Series.
QA276.8 .F73 2002
519.5′44—dc21
                                                    2001008013

Editorial Credits
Susan Evento, Managing Editor/Product Development; Elizabeth Jaffe, Senior Editor; Sydney Wright and Charles Hunt, Designers; Kimberly Danger and Heide Schoof, Photo Researchers

Photo Credits
Cover: Palma Allen; Title Page: Esbin-Anderson/Photo Network (top left), Karen Holsinger Mullen/Unicorn Stock (top right), David F. Clobes (bottom left), Debra Turnrose (bottom right); Page 4: Index Stock; Page 5: Esbin-Anderson/Photo Network; Page 6: Dusty Willison/International Stock; Page 7: Michael Keller/Uniphoto; Page 8: Karen Holsinger Mullen/Unicorn Stock; Page 9: David F. Clobes; Page 10: Jack Glisson/Kentucky Up Close; Page 11: Debra Turnrose; Page 12: Photri-Microstock; Page 13: Debra Turnrose; Page 14: Richard Price/FPG International; Page 15: Valerie Lewis/Picture Cube; Page 16: David F. Clobes; Page 17: David F. Clobes; Page 18: Jack Glisson/Kentucky Up Close

Table of Contents

Estimating is making
a close guess.
We estimate when we do not
need to be exact.

We can use
our eyes
to estimate
about how
much salad
will fit
in the bowl.

But when we bake, we need
to measure exact amounts,
so the muffins come out right.

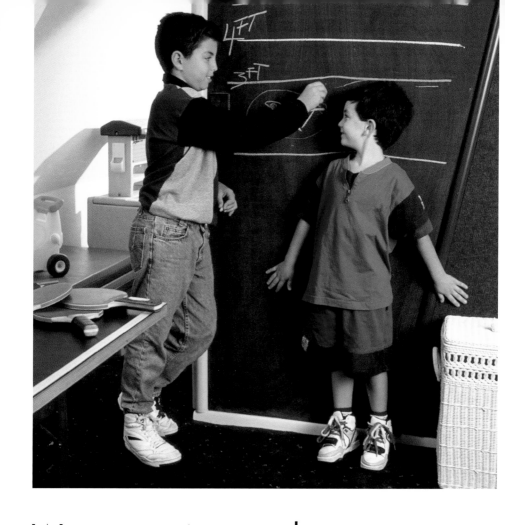

We can estimate when
we measure how tall we are.
Our eyes are a good tool
to make an estimate.

Sometimes we need to know an exact measurement. A doctor measures us with a very long ruler to get our exact height.

We can use our eyes
and hands to estimate
how far apart to plant
each vegetable.

But when we build a bird feeder,
we need to be exact.
We measure the wood
with a ruler.

Sometimes we use a ruler
to estimate.
With a ruler, we can see
that the paper
is about 1 foot long
or a little longer than 1 foot.

We can estimate using measuring tools like our own feet. This line is about 10 of her feet long!

Our hungry stomachs
help us estimate
how much cereal
we can eat for breakfast.

We can estimate how many
candies are in the first glass.
There are 20 candies
in the second glass.
Can you estimate how many
candies are in the first glass?

It can be fun to estimate.
We can estimate
how many steps it will take
to get down the hill.

We can estimate
how many steps it will take
to catch up with the ball.

We can estimate
the cost of things.
One jar is 49¢.
That is about 50¢.
Estimate how many jars
you can get for 100¢.

Before we go outside, we can
estimate the temperature
by putting our hands
out the window.
Now we know what to wear.

We can all estimate when we do not need to be exact!

When is it helpful for you to estimate?

Glossary

cost—the price of an item

estimate—to make a guess

exact—correct and accurate, not a guess

fit—to have the right size and shape

guess—an answer that you do not know for sure is right

height—to measure how tall or high something is

longer—having more length

measure—to find out the size of something in units

ruler—a flat stick used for measuring length and height

temperature—how hot or cold something is

Index/Word List

Word Count: 317
Early-Intervention Level: 16